RECORDED VERSIONS
GUITAR

AUTHENTIC TRANSCRIPTIONS
WITH NOTES & TABLATURE
Transcribed by
LENNY CARLSON
Edited by
FRED SOKOLOW

John Lee Ho
A Blues Le...

CW00542054

CONTENTS

ISBN 0-7935-0310-8

ARC
MUSIC
GROUP

EXCLUSIVELY DISTRIBUTED BY

HAL•LEONARD®
CORPORATION
7777 W. BLUEMOUND RD. P.O. BOX 13819 MILWAUKEE, WI 53213

JOHN LEE HOOKER
A Blues Legend

Post World War II America was starting to roll peacefully forward when John Lee Hooker's hard, electric blues hit the ground running. Raised in Detroit, his stark, steelyard blues pounded and clanged with the grinding intensity of Ford's assembly line, even as their context and modal forms drifted back to the Delta haze of depression era Mississippi. The raw, over-amplified guitar tone which Chicago Blues pioneer Muddy Waters used to slice through drum driven, juke joint dances, became the primary instrumental voice, possessing a physicality and sensuousness that was as pure as Abstract Expressionist Jackson Pollock's drip paintings of the late 40's.

As the global horrors of war obliterated rural America's pastoral innocence, the economic incentives of steady employment in defense plants induced mass migration from the South. The metallic noise of the northern factory towns was the clarion call for blue collar workers as well as musicians, artists, and writers. Out of this urban mind warp stimulation came John Lee's butt-bangin' boogie and brutal amp distortion, foreshadowing the rhythm and rage of the Rock 'n Roll that would follow.

The Hook was born on August 22, 1917 in Clarksdale, Mississippi, the birthplace of many of the greatest Delta blues men including Charlie Patton, Robert Johnson, Muddy Waters, Big Joe Williams and Son House. His stepfather, Will Moore, taught him to play and was his primary influence along with Tommy McClennan. He moved to Memphis while in his teens where he performed with slide guitar stylist Robert Nighthawk and sang gospel music. By 1943, he was living in the Motor City, pushing a broom on the day shift and pulling deep blues out of his amplified Stella guitar at night.

1948 was the official birth of the term "Rhythm & Blues." RCA Victor retired the pejorative "Race Music" label in favor of the new classification for black music, as did *Billboard* magazine one year later. Waiting to help define this new style, like a junk yard dog straining at its chain, were Hooker's "Sally Mae" and "Boogie Chillun," on the Modern label. "Boogie Chillun," with its hard rockin' shuffle beat (kicked along by Hooker's tapping feet), racksaw guitar tone and rolling I chord riff, was as vital to the development of R & B as Muddy Waters' "I Can't Be Satisfied" (also released in 1948), was to Chicago Blues.

40 years of recording on a dozen different labels under a gaggle of pseudonyms followed, with most of the initial sessions featuring Hooker flying solo. Second guitarists Andrew Dunham and Eddie Kirkland, in addition to harp player Eddie Burns, appeared on some cuts between 1948 and 1950. Beginning in 1951, however, full rhythm sections (as a bow to commercial considerations) became the rule as John Lee's lone troubadour persona receded. Chicago-style recordings followed until the early sixties when folkies "discovered" his music and welcomed his solo acoustic guitar or politely amplified electric. From the mid-sixties until the present, he has again recorded almost exclusively with small ensembles.

Hooker is probably the most recorded bluesman ever, with his vinyl output weighing in at over 100 albums. In addition, he has enjoyed the presence of a veritable blues all-star team of sidemen. The first string (Hooker is a big baseball fan) would include his cousin Earl Hooker, Eddie Taylor, Jimmy Reed, T-Bone Walker, Willie Dixon, Otis Spann, Muddy Waters, Wayne Bennett, Phil Upchurch, Lowell Fulson, Robert Cray, Charlie Musselwhite, Bonnie Raitt, Canned Heat and rockers Carlos Santana, Los Lobos, and Steve Miller.

John Lee Hooker's hip shakin', neck snappin' boogies and I chord, slow blues excursions are some of the most original and important contributions made to the R & B vocabulary. His stone sober, talking vocals and whisky & women lyrics have influenced singers from Eric Burdon to George Thorogood. When rockers in the sixties made *their* discovery of the blues, Hooker's boogie patterns became the jam of choice, with Canned Heat building their live act around various "Refried Boogies." Norman Greenbaum's "Spirit In The Sky," Z.Z. Top's "LaGrange" and most recently Joe Satriani's "Satch's Boogie" all owe their I, $\flat III$, IV lick to the boogie man. Most significantly, Hooker's haunting, modal blues and tube torturing distortion had a profound effect on Jimi Hendrix. "Voodoo Child," "Voodoo Chile (Slight Return)" and "Hear My Train A 'Comin" are the most obvious examples, but a rock tune like "In From The Storm," besides being based on a repetitive blues lick, has the same call and response, guitar/vocal dialogue as Hooker classics like "Crawling Kig Snake."

Along with Muddy Waters and Howlin' Wolf, the Hook casts a giant shadow that covers the Delta Blues of the 30's, the primal electric R & B of the late 40's and eclectic blendings of 60's rock and beyond. His free form and liquid meter are hypnotic as they compress and expand the perception of time while his images of infidelity are as pointed as a punch in the eye. And yes, those bumping, pumping boogies can still fire up the rampant randiness of anyone who "has the boogie-woogie in 'em that's got to come out."

JOHN LEE HOOKER
Guitar Style

John Lee Hooker grew up in the Mississippi Delta region, birthplace of most of the blues giants in this century. Learning guitar from his stepfather at the age of twelve, he forged a simple, unique and powerful style of his own.

Whether he's playing solo acoustic guitar or electric and fronting an eight-piece band with a horn section, Hooker always sounds like the real thing: the original Delta blues sound, and about as close to the source as you can get.

RIGHT HAND PICKING STYLE

Hooker's picking is unconventional. Like many blues players, he uses his thumb and fingers and wears no picks. Sometimes he fingerpicks in typical blues fashion, playing a fairly consistent droning bass with his thumb, and picking melody notes with his fingers, as in these examples:

from *DOWN AT THE LANDING*

from *BOTTLE UP AND GO*

More often, he plays a rhythmic thumb-and-finger riff to back up his voice, then interrupts the riff (and stops the thumb/bass for lead breaks or fills. In slow blues ballads like *MY FIRST WIFE LEFT ME, TUPELO, WEDNESDAY EVENING BLUES* and *THE MIGHTY FIRE*, this creates a very sparse texture. It's even sparser when (on these slower tunes) he stops playing entirely but keeps his foot tapping and interjects single-note solos and riffs *between* vocals.

Here are some of the lively rhythmic riffs Hooker plays to accompany his boogie tunes:

from *BOTTLE UP AND GO*

from *LEAVE MY WIFE ALONE*

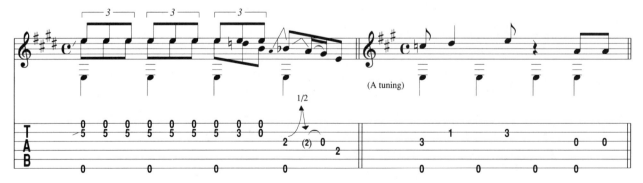

Some of Hooker's solos include rhythmic chord bashing
passages played by thumb downstrokes. The chords are often
dominant sevenths and the rhythm is often in triplet patterns:

from WEDNESDAY EVENING BLUES   **from MY FIRST WIFE LEFT ME**   **from BOTTLE UP AND GO**

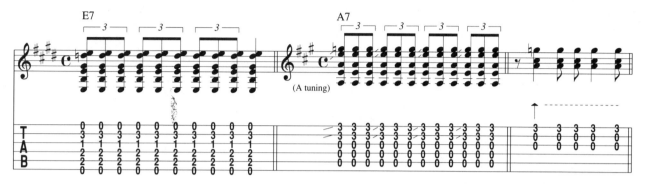

Look for other examples of chord-bashing solos in *CANAL
STREET BLUES, LEAVE MY WIFE ALONE* and the introduction
to *PROCESS.*

PLAYING IN THE KEY OF E

When he's not playing boogie tunes in open tuning, Hooker
almost always plays in standard tuning in the key of E. Except
for occasional forays up the neck on the top two strings, he
stays within the typical E blues scale:

Here are some of the common key-of-E slides, chokes and
pull-offs Hooker frequently uses:

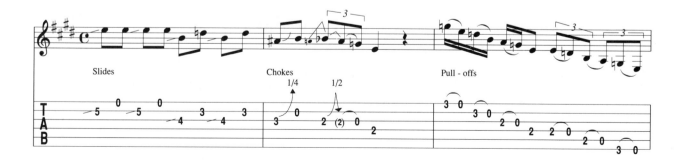

Trills are an important part of Hooker's sound, especially on
slow blues like *IT SERVES ME RIGHT TO SUFFER, BLUES
BEFORE SUNRISE* and *THE MIGHTY FIRE.* Here are the trills
he plays most often:

Often, Hooker plays a repetitious, one or two bar single-
note riff to back up his singing. Here are some samples:

from *BOOM, BOOM, BOOM*   **from *WEDNESDAY EVENING BLUES***

from *CATFISH*

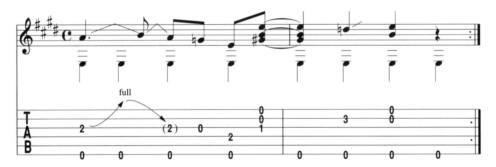

In addition to his single-note soloing and chord soloing,
Hooker interjects some two-string chord fragments. Here
are his favorites:

from *DOWN AT THE LANDING*   **from *DIMPLES***

OPEN A AND G TUNINGS

Hooker plays many of his boogies — and an occasional slow blues — in open G or A tunings. The strings are tuned the same in A tuning as in G tuning, only a whole step (two frets) higher; so scales, fingering and chords are identical in the two tunings. Once you've learned a tune in open G tuning, you can play it exactly the same way in open A; the effect will be the same as playing it in open G with a capo on the second fret.

G tuning	A tuning	
D	E	1
B	C♯	2
G	A	3
D	E	4
G	A	5
D	E	6

TO GET TO OPEN G TUNING FROM STANDARD TUNING:

•Tune the 1st and 6th strings down to D; match them with the open 4th string/D.

•Tune the 5th string down to G; match it with the open 3rd string/G.

TO GET TO OPEN A TUNING FROM STANDARD TUNING:

•Tune the 4th string up to E; match it with the open 1st and 6th string/E

•Tune the 3rd string up to A; match it with the open 5th string/A.

•Tune the 2nd string up to Cs; match it with the (re-tuned) 3rd string/4th fret.

CHORDS: Hooker seldom plays chord changes when in open tuning, except for the seventh chord shown above. Occasionally he uses the IV chord (also shown above). In G tuning, it's a C chord and in A tuning, it's a D chord.

Here's a blues scale Hooker uses in G tuning; use the same fingering in A tuning for an A blues scale:

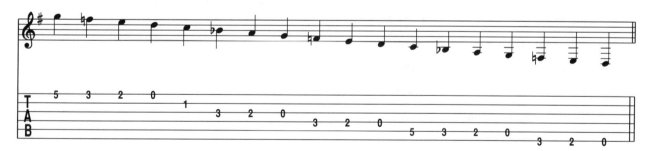

Here are some typical Hooker slides, pull-offs and chokes in open G, plus some double-note licks he often plays:

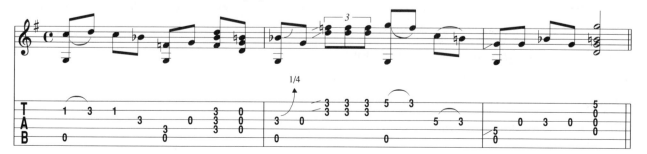

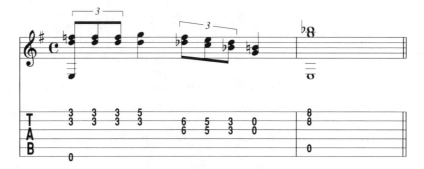

The open tuning songs in this collection are *BOTTLE UP AND GO, MY FIRST WIFE LEFT ME, CANAL STREET BLUES,* and *LEAVE MY WIFE ALONE* (open A), and *STELLA MAE* and *ONE BOURBON, ONE SCOTCH, ONE BEER* (open G).

THE PRIMITIVE BLUES

Though Hooker plays in urban situations, often with an electric band that includes another guitar, bass, drums, keyboard and several horns, his playing harks back to an earlier rural blues style. The original blues, as played in the latter part of the nineteenth century, was unencumbered by chord changes and free of the restriction of an eight or twelve-bar format. The older strains of the blues tradition are strong in Hooker's playing, and he is as free and improvisational a blues player as can be found. In live performances and recording sessions, he often makes up tunes on the spot!

CHORDS: In some of his solo performances, Hooker stays on the tonic chord throughout (*THE MIGHTY FIRE, BOTTLE UP AND GO and MY FIRST WIFE LEFT ME,* for example). Sometimes the band plays chord changes based on cues from Hooker's vocals — with unorthodox results (listen to *ONE BOURBON, ONE SCOTCH, ONE BEER* and *STELLA MAE*). Other times, as in *BLUES BEFORE SUNRISE,* the band relentlessly repeats the twelve bar blues pattern while Hooker vocalizes freely, ending and beginning verses in the middle of the twelve-bar chorus, or stretching a lyric to resolve a verse with the band. In all these situations, Hooker is in control, doing it *his* way.

RHYTHM: Without regard to conventional form, Hooker adds beats and extends bars as he pleases, which explains all the bars of 2/4, 5/4 and 6/4 time sprinkled throughout these 4/4 tunes. These occur during vocals as well as solos. See, for example, *THE MIGHTY FIRE, BOTTLE UP AND GO, ONE BOURBON, ONE SCOTCH, ONE BEER, CATFISH BLUES* and *DOWN AT THE LANDING.*

There are other unpredictable and unusual touches throughout Hooker's music. To name just a few:

• In *MY FIRST WIFE LEFT ME* he plays a long, unothodox bass solo on the 5th and 6th strings.

• In the same tune, he repeatedly plays an oddly-voiced D7 chord:

(A tuning)

• In *WEDNESDAY EVENING BLUES* he simultaneously sings and plays the same line. This is a common blues device, but unusual for Hooker.

• He scat sings at the end of *LEAVE MY WIFE ALONE.*

The twenty tunes transcribed in this book — and Hooker's work in general — are well worth studying. They are powerful blues performances by one of the last original blues players, a link to the roots of blues music. And today, when guitar pyrotechnics are so much in the spotlight, Hooker's music, which comes directly from the man's heart and soul and guts, preaches a message of honesty and deep feeling.

Boom Boom

By John Lee Hooker

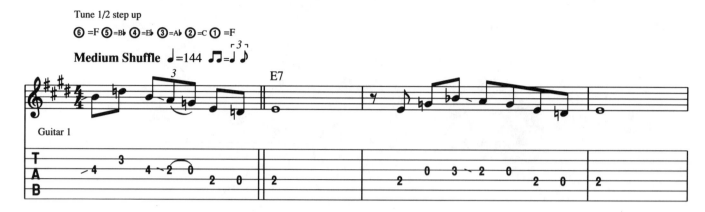

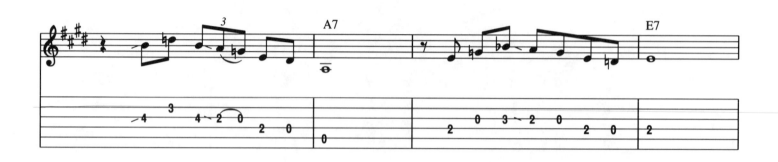

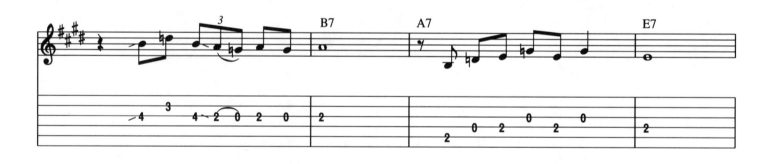

1. Boom, boom, boom, boom.   Gon-na shoot you right down.

2., 3. *See additional lyrics*

Instrumental break

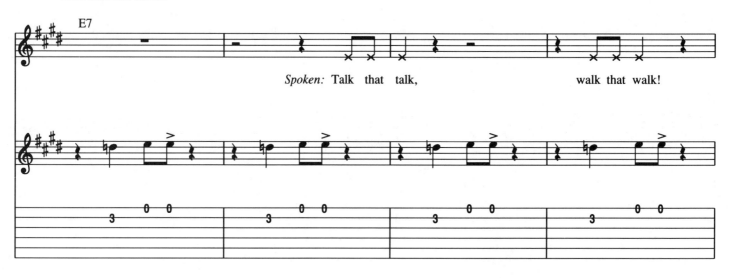

Spoken: Talk that talk, walk that walk!

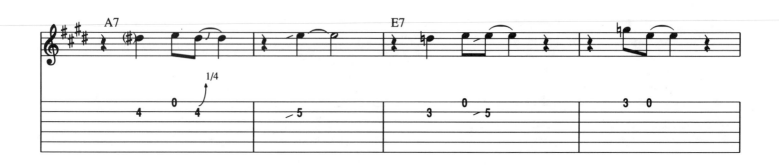

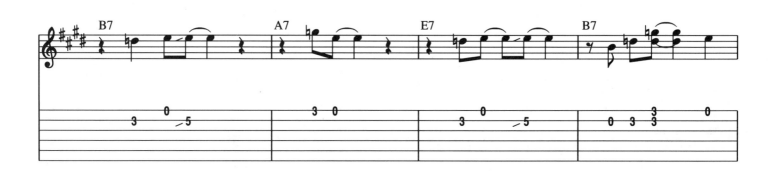

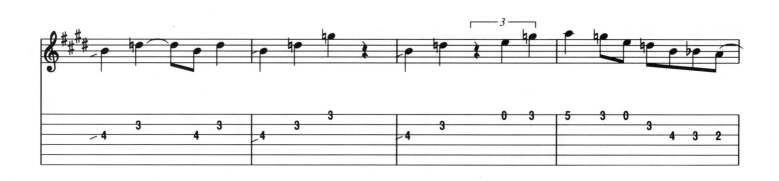

D.S. (3rd verse) and Fade

Repeat ad lib. 5 times

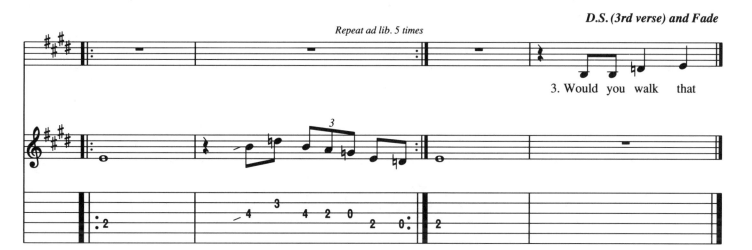

3. Would you walk that

2nd Verse
Oh, ho, ho, ho
Mm, mm, mm
Mm, mm, mm
I love to see you strut
Up and down the floor,
When you're talkin' to me
That baby talk.
I like it like that
Whoa, yeah *(lead into solo)*

3rd verse
Sung: Would you walk that walk,
And talk that talk?
And whisper in my ear
Tell me that you love me
Spoken: I love that talk
When you talk like that
You knock me out
Right off of my feet

(Fade out)

Whoa, walk that walk, talk that talk, etc.

Bottle Up And Go

By John Lee Hooker

Tuning:

⑥ =E ⑤=A ④ =E ③=A ②=C♯ ① =E

Medium Blues tempo ♩ = 108-120

1. Well   Ma - ma killed a chick - en   thought it was a duck;   you
   may be   old,   you might be   grey;   you

3. *(See additional lyrics)*

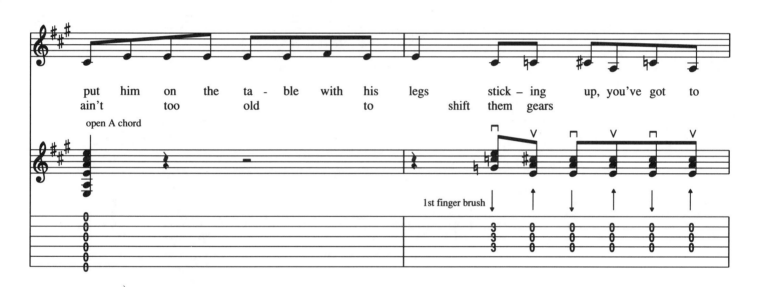

put him   on   the   ta - ble   with   his   legs   stick – ing   up, you've got   to
ain't   too   old   to   shift   them   gears   you

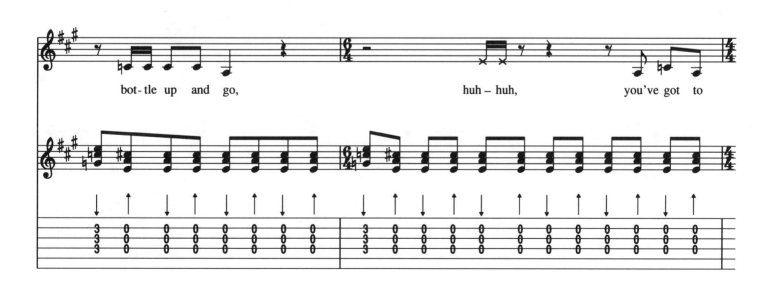

bot - tle up and go,   huh – huh,   you've got   to

Spoken: When you say it   now gui-tar,

Instrumental break

say it   for me.

continue with similar licks

(pull with thumb)

slide up string, then down

18

3. Well, a

⊕ *Coda*

Well, you high - pow - ered wom - en

Fine

sure got to bor - row love and go bop! bop! bop! bop! bop! bop!

3rd verse:
Well, a nickel is a nickel
Dime is a dime
A houseful of kids
And now she's mine

(Substitute last chorus)

You've got to get out of here, woman
You've got to get out of here, woman *(to coda)*

Blues Before Sunrise

By John Lee Hooker

Electric Guitar
tune up 1/2 step

⑥=F ⑤=B♭ ④=E♭ ③=A♭ ②=C ①=F

Slow Blues ♫ = ♩ ♪

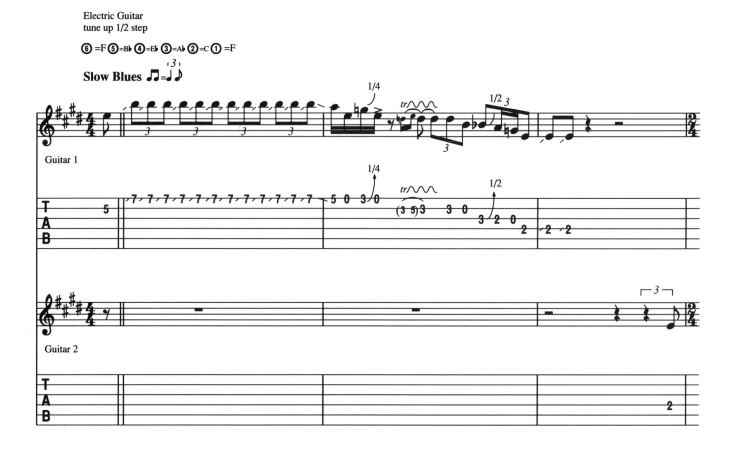

Guitar 1

Guitar 2

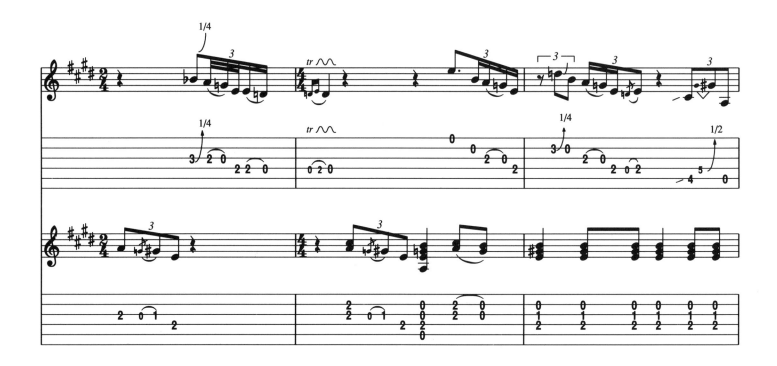

Instrumental

boys, I do de - spise.

Yes,   yes

Guitar 2

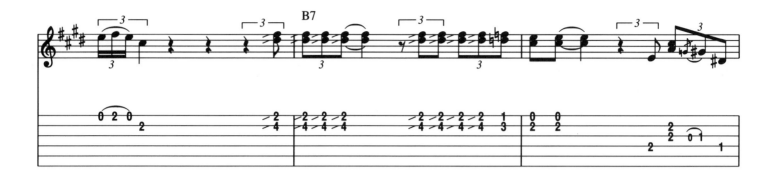

D.S. al Coda ⊕

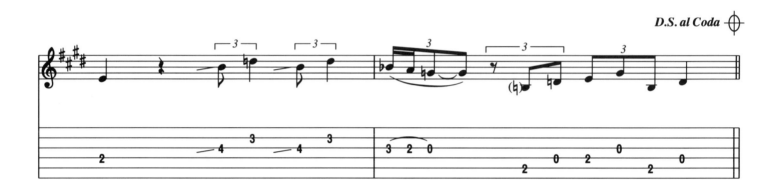

⊕ *Coda*

Blues be – fore sun – rise, tears in my eyes.____

3rd verse
Lost everything, everything I ever owned;
Lost everything, everything I ever owned.
For seven long years, I tried to get along.
(Coda) Blues before sunrise, tears standing in my eyes.

Canal Street Blues

By John Lee Hooker

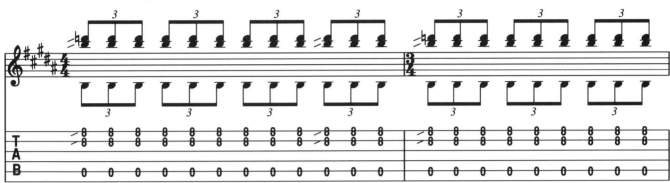

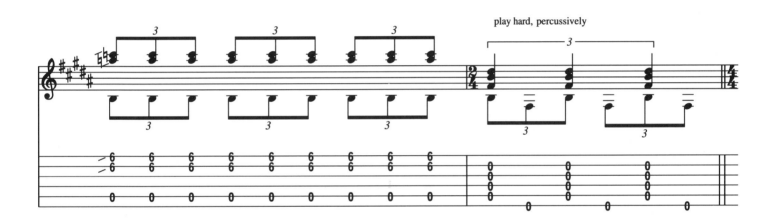

- key's   stream-ing just like wine. _

Tell me   down ____ in New Or–leans. _____

Whis - key's stream-in' just like wine. _

Instrumental

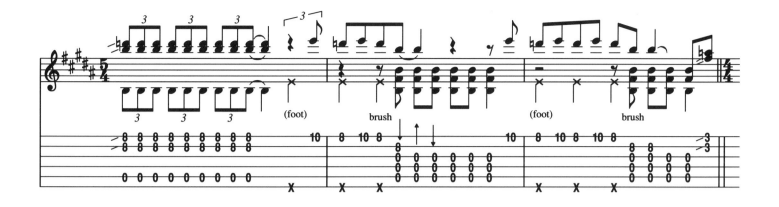

D.S. al Coda

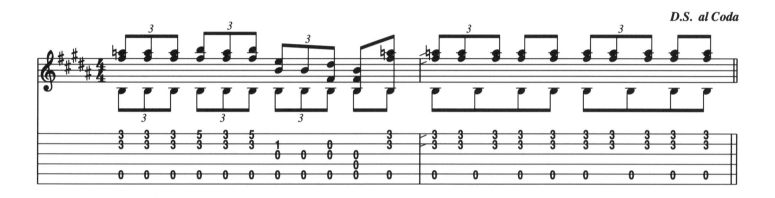

Coda

Fine

Keep on, down in New Or- leans.

(foot)

brush w/thumb

brush

2nd verse
They tell me Canal Street is the longest street in town.
They tell me Canal Street is the longest street in town.
Yes, you ride all day long, you're still on Canal Street.

3rd verse
Then they tell me again, people (Lord, have mercy!)
It's the widest street in town.
Then they tell me again, it's the widest street in town.
Lord, I'm just gonna keep on riding,
(Coda) Keep on, down in New Orleans.

Catfish

By John Lee Hooker

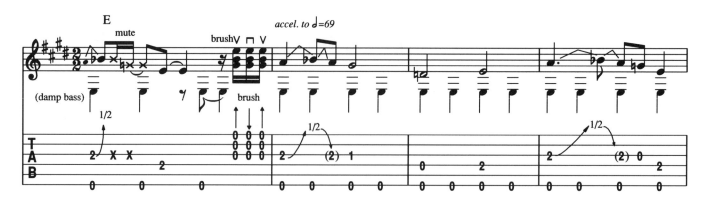

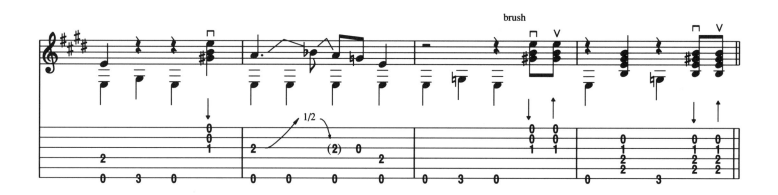

1. Yes,   I   wish   I   was   a

2. Yes,   I   went   down   to   the

3.,4.,5. *(See additonal lyrics)*

3rd verse
Yes, I went to my baby's house.
And I sat down on her step.
She said, "Come on in, now, Johnny,
Oh, Lord, my husband just now left."
Husband just now left...
Sure enough just, sure enough, just now left.
Sure enough just...

4th verse
"Got something to tell you, Oh Lord, baby.
Baby you know that ain't right.
You cook cornbread for your husband
And biscuits for your man."
Biscuits for your man, biscuits for your man.
Biscuits for your man, biscuits for your man.

5th verse
Oh Lord, Oh Lord, baby,
Lord you know I'm going away.
Yes, I'm going away now, now, now, baby, Oh Lord.
Crying won't make, crying won't make,
Crying won't make me stay.

Dimples

By John Lee Hooker and James Bracken

1. I ___ love the way you walk.
2. I ___ like the way you switch.
3. You've got dim-ples in your jaws.
4. Well, I see you ev-'ry-day.

I ___ love the way you
I ___ like the way you
You've got dim-ples in your
Well I see your ev-'ry

To Coda ⊕

B

I _____	love	the	way	you	walk;
I _____	like	the	way	you	switch;
You've got	dim – ples	in	your	jaws
Well, I	see	you	ev – 'ry	day

you're my   babe ___

1., 2., 3.

E

___ I've got my eye on you.

tr ∿∿∿∿

Instrumental Break

Last time,D.S. al Coda ✛

Play 6 times

✛ *Coda*

Fine

I've got my eye on you.

(Bass run adapted from string bass part)

Down At The Landing

By John Lee Hooker

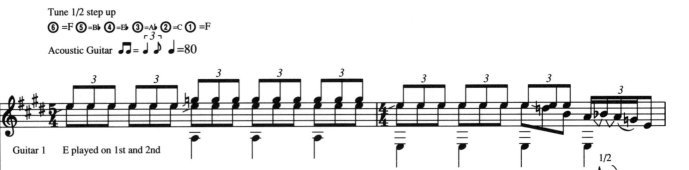

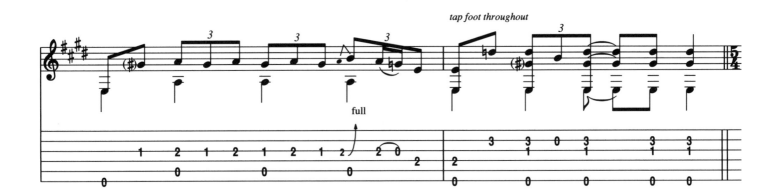

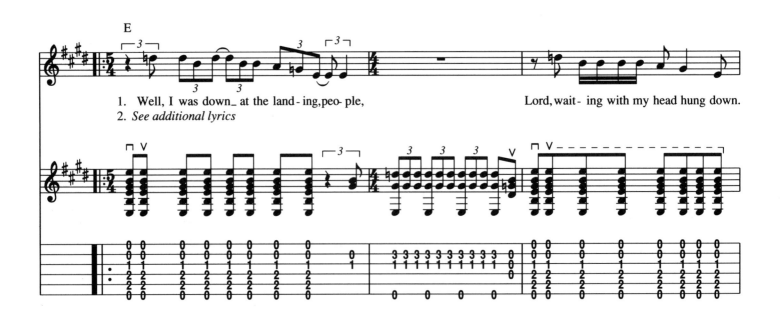

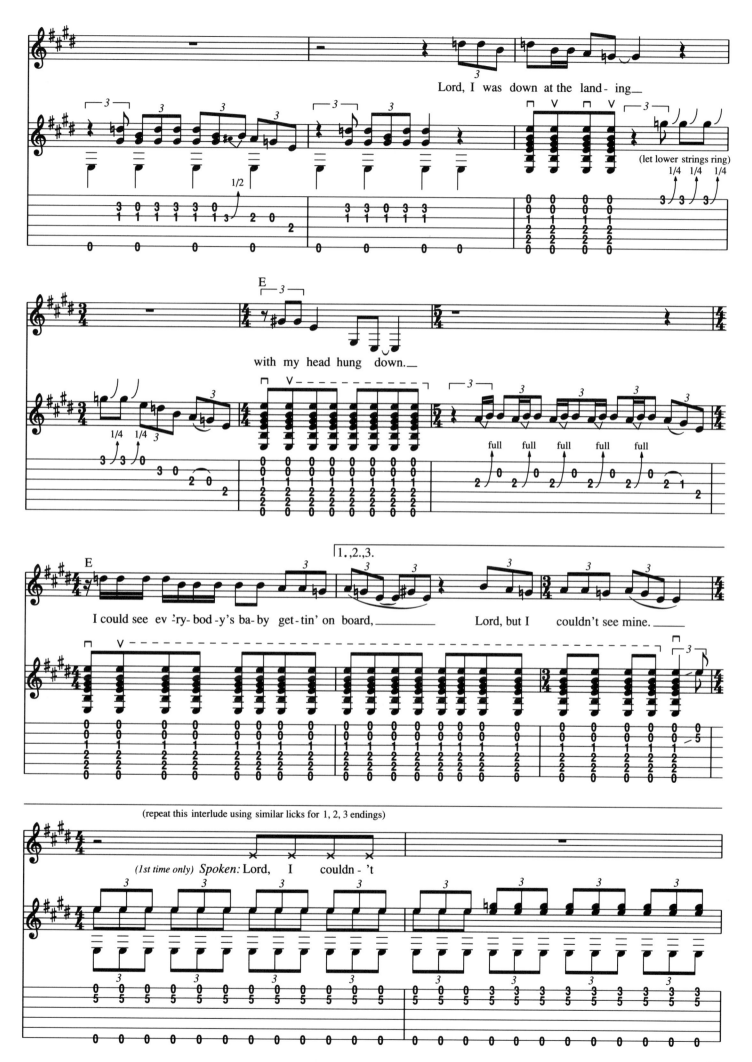

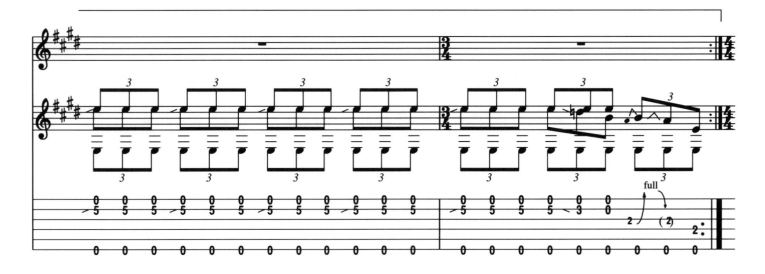

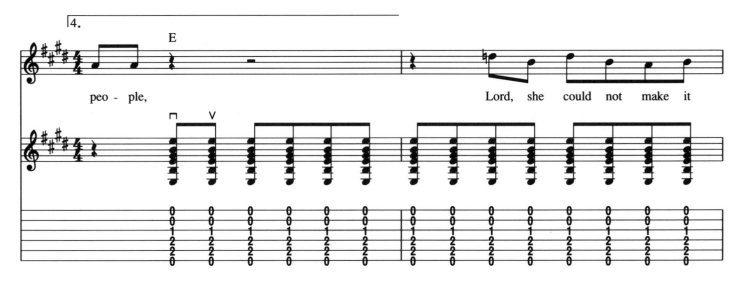

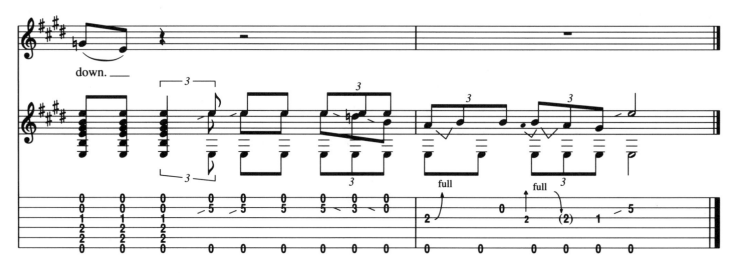

2nd verse
I said, "Lord, have mercy. Where could my baby be?"
I said, "Lord, have mercy. Where could my baby be?"
I see everybody's baby, baby, baby,
But I can't see mine.

3rd verse
The big boat kept on rolling,
Big boat kept on rolling along.
(Spoken) Lord, but it did.
Lord, the big boat, the big boat, people;
Big boat kept on rolling along.
I was standing there wondering, with my
head hung down.

4th verse
I believe I'll call to Chicago (yes, yes, yes);
I'm gonna seize my baby down.
Oh, call to Chicago, seize my baby down.
My baby might've got hung up, people,
(Last ending) Lord, she couldn't make it down

It Serves Me Right To Suffer

By John Lee Hooker

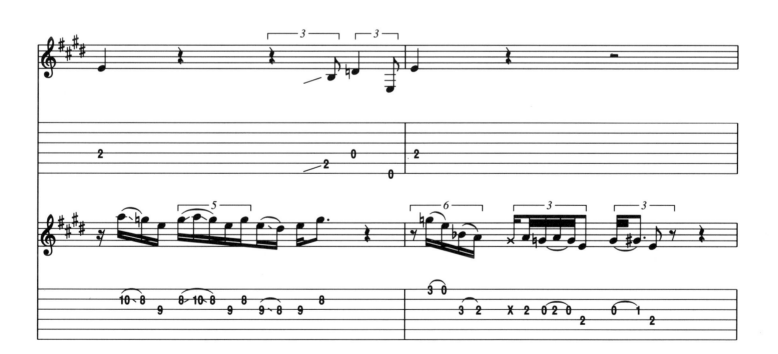

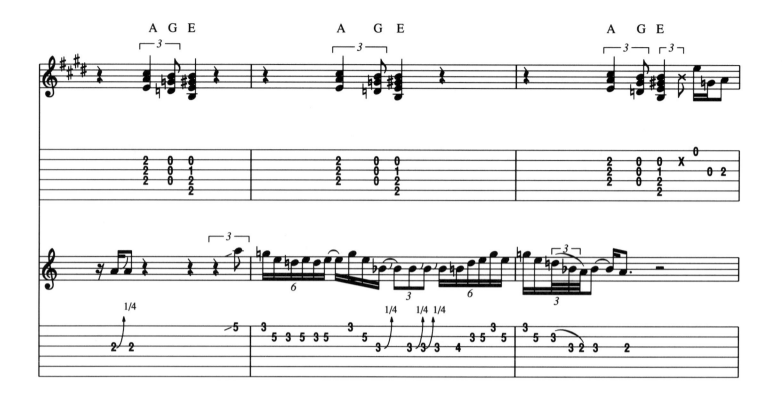

1. It serves me right to suf-fer,__   it serves me right

2.,3. *See additional lyrics*

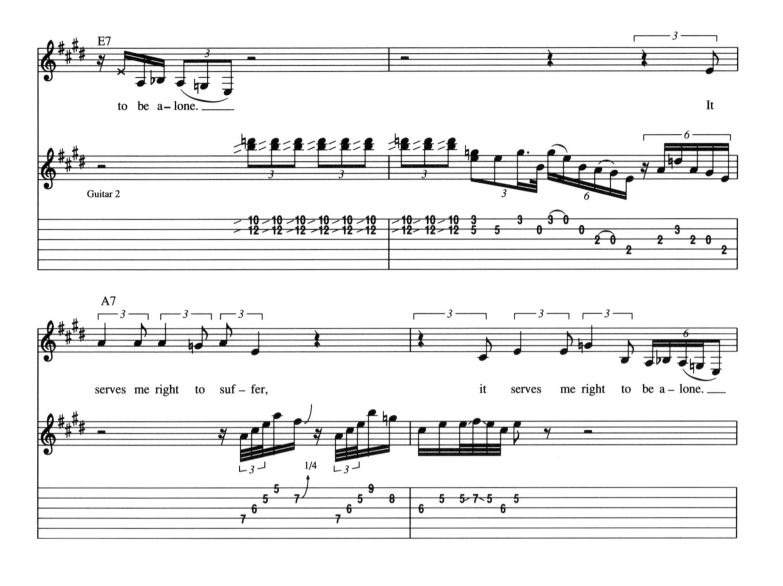

to be a–lone. _____

It

Guitar 2

serves me right   to suf–fer,   it   serves   me right   to be a–lone. ___

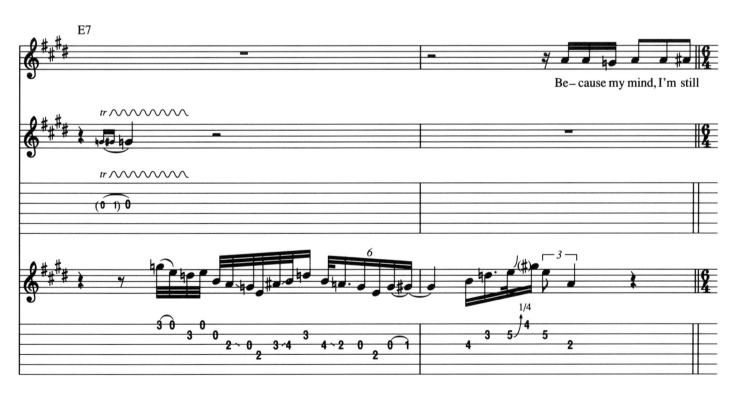

Be–cause my mind, I'm still

liv – ing,   the days   done passed and gone.___

Instrumental break

Fade

(muted chords)

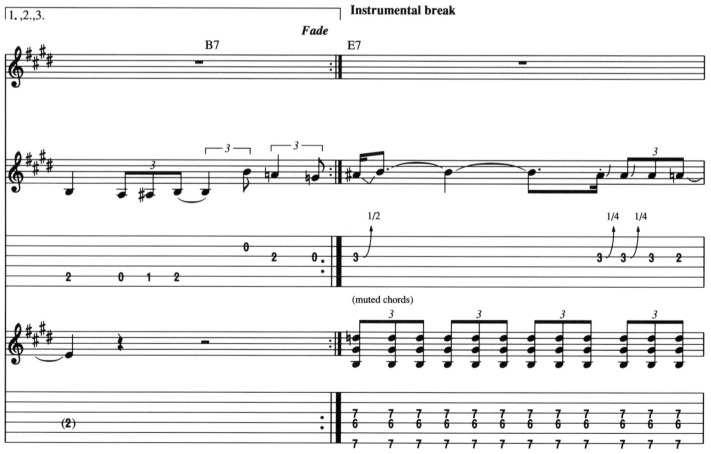

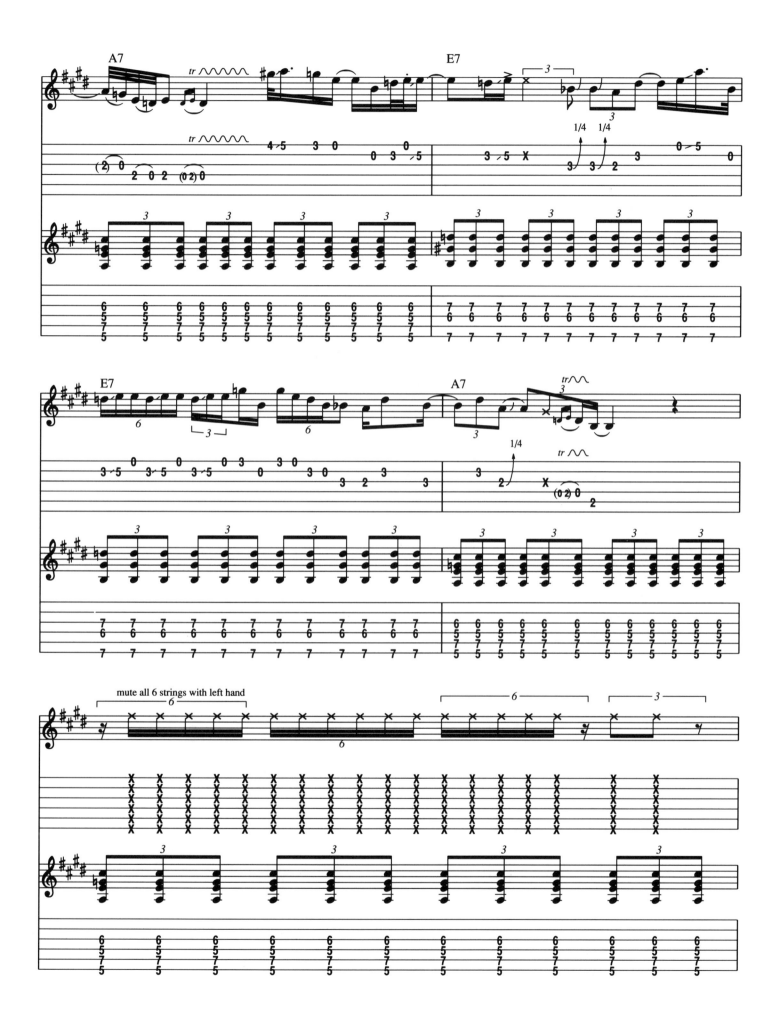

2nd Verse:
Everytime I see a woman,
And, folks, she makes me think of mine.
Every time I see a woman,
And, folks, she makes me think of mine.
And that's why, that's why
Folks, I just can't keep from crying.

3rd Verse:
My doctor put me on
Milk, cream and alcohol.
My doctor put me on, put me on,
Milk, cream and alcohol.
He said, "Johnny, your nerves are so bad,
So bad, Johnny, until you just can't
Sleep at night." (Oh yes, oh yes)

Repeat 1st verse and fade.

Leave My Wife Alone

By John Lee Hooker

open tuning
⑥ =E ⑤=A ④ =E ③=A ②=C# ①=E
capo 1st fret
Fast Shuffle Blues ♩=176-192
Acoustic Guitar

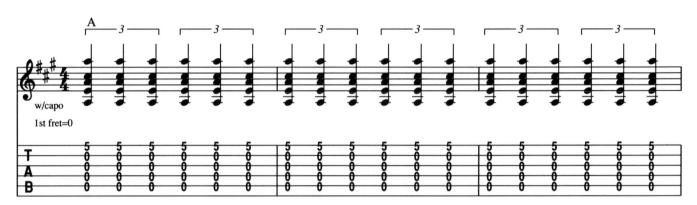

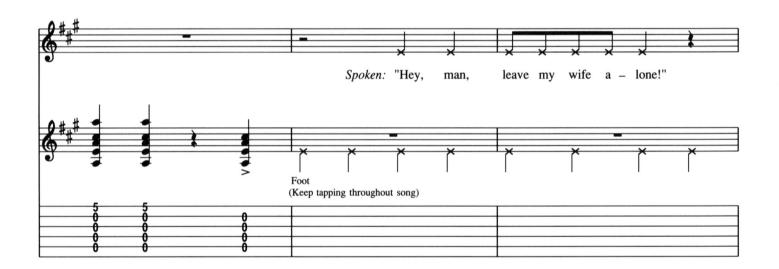

Spoken: "Hey, man, leave my wife a – lone!"

Foot
(Keep tapping throughout song)

brush
(let ring)

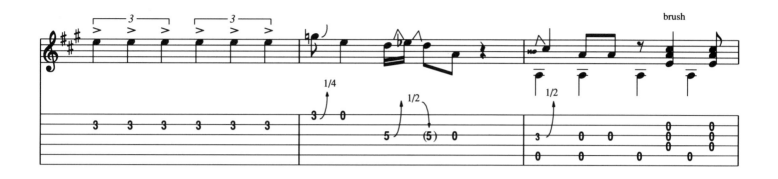

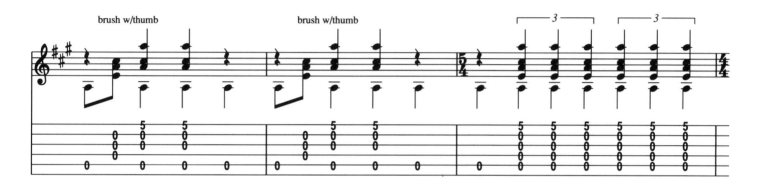

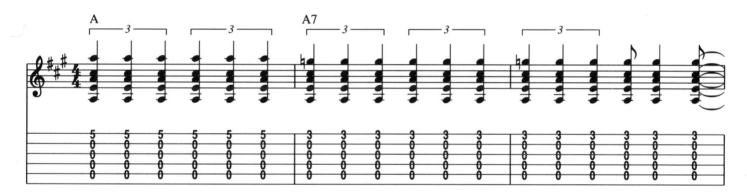

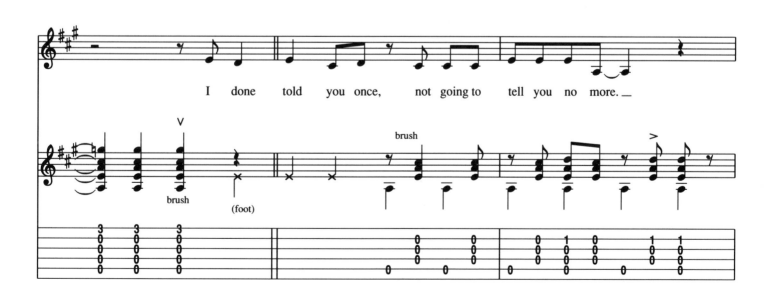

I done told you once, not going to tell you no more. ___

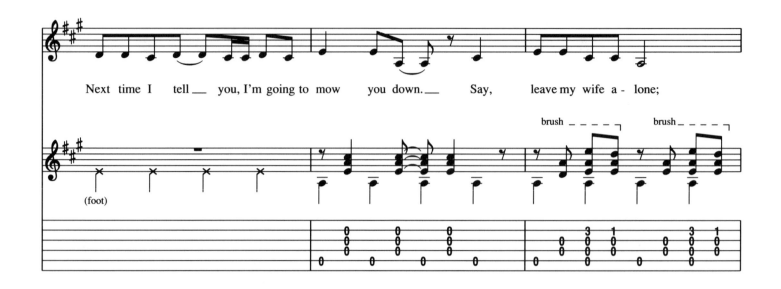

Next time I tell ___ you, I'm going to mow ___ you down. ___ Say, leave my wife a - lone;

(foot)

say leave her a - lone. I said,

(foot)

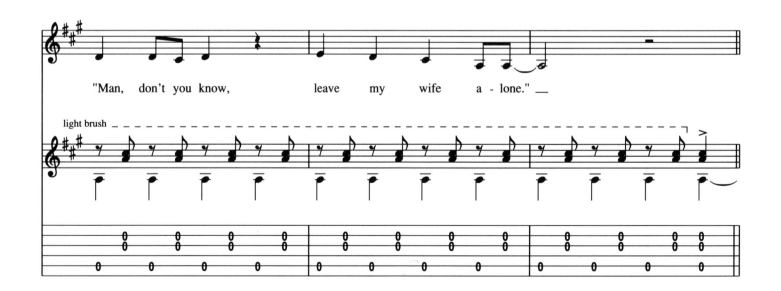

"Man, don't you know, leave my wife a - lone." ___

Instrumental

(let ring)

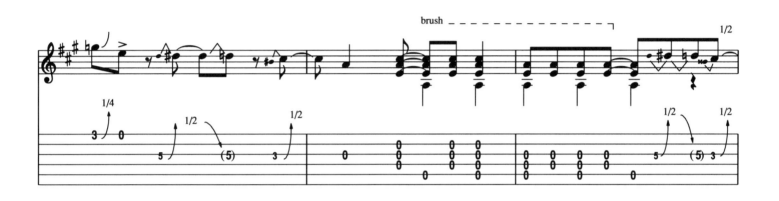

brush

1/4   1/2   1/2   1/2   1/2

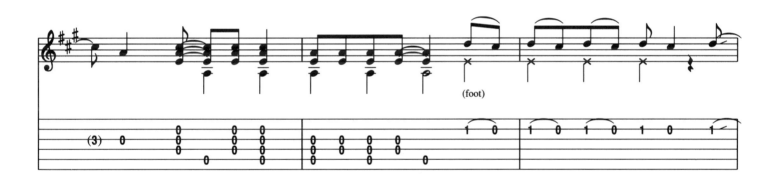

(foot)

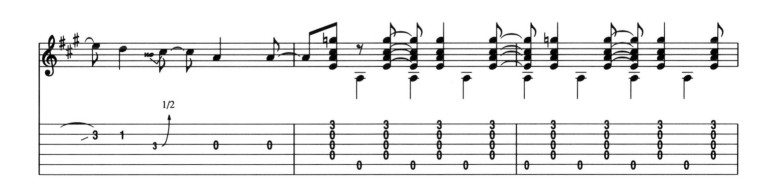

1/2

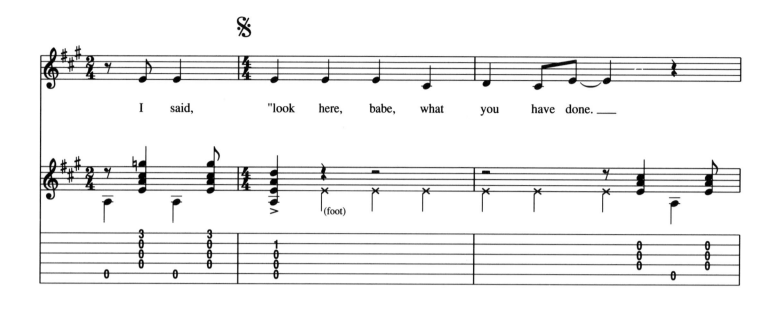

I said, "look here, babe, what you have done. ___

Got my love ___ and got me on a bun." Ba- by, leave him a- lone.
                I have told you, ba- by; ___

Ba – by leave him a- lone.   I done
I done told you, ba -- by.   I done

told you   once, ___   not going to tell you no more. ___
told you,   ba - by   leave that man   a - lone. ___

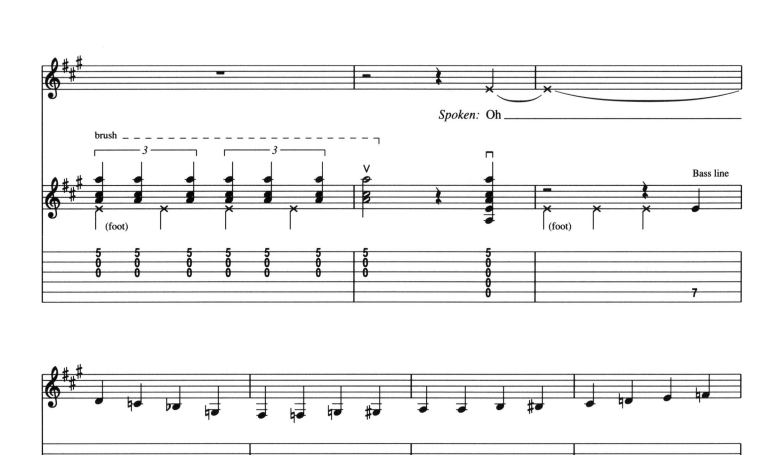

Spoken: Oh ____

Spoken: Oh, ____ have mer- cy!

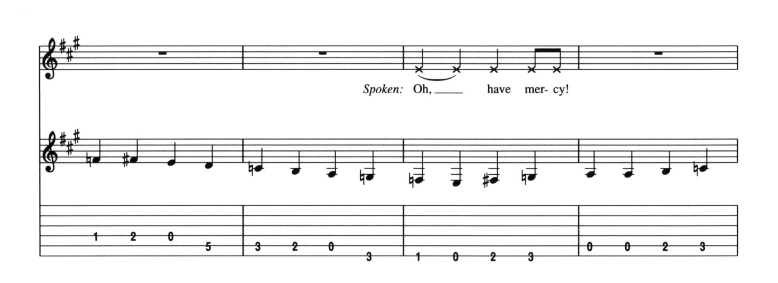

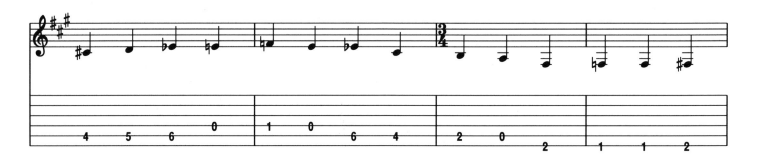

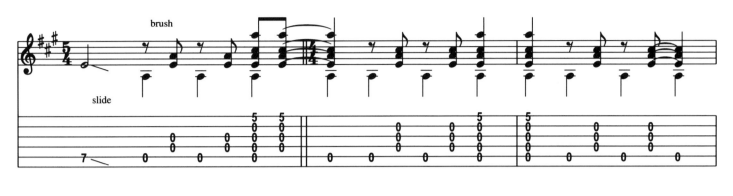

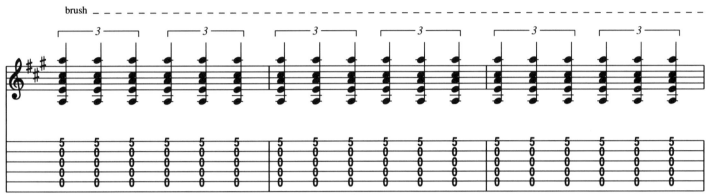

D.S. al Coda ⊕

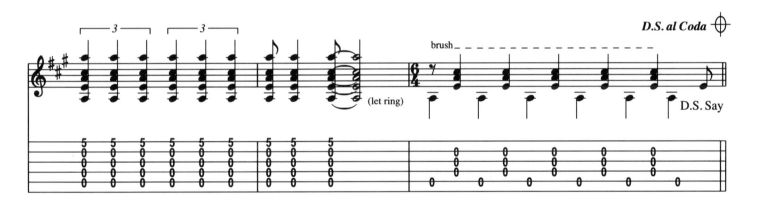

⊕ **Coda**

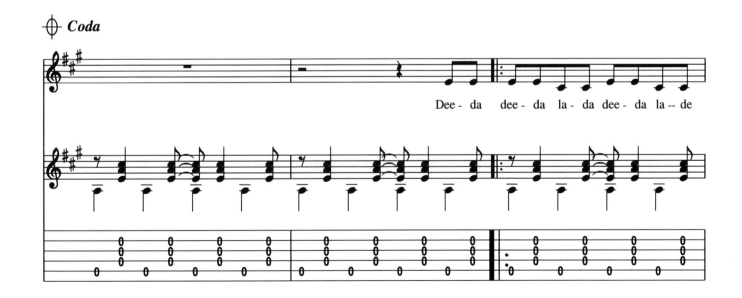

Dee - da dee - da la - da dee - da la -- de

dee- da la- da lo- da, dee- da "Ba - by, now,   ba- by,   leave that   man   a - lone." _
    I   said,

foot   (keep tapping)

brush

damp bass

Fine

One Bourbon, One Scotch, One Beer

By John Lee Hooker

Moderate Blues Shuffle ♩=108

Open G tuning: ⑥=D ⑤=G ④=D ③=G ②=B ①=D

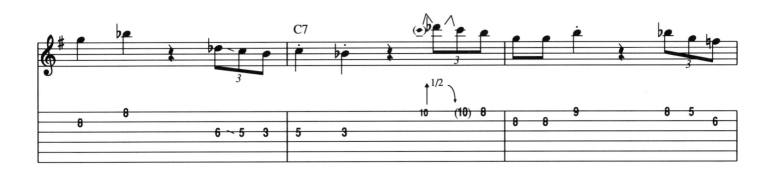

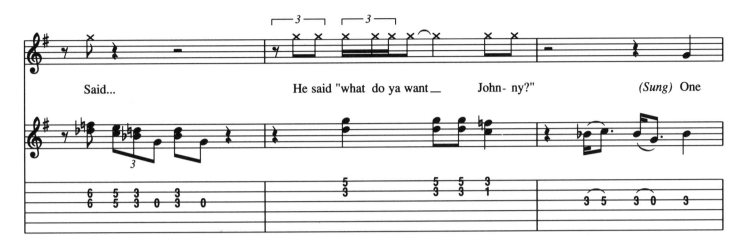

2nd time D.S. and Fade

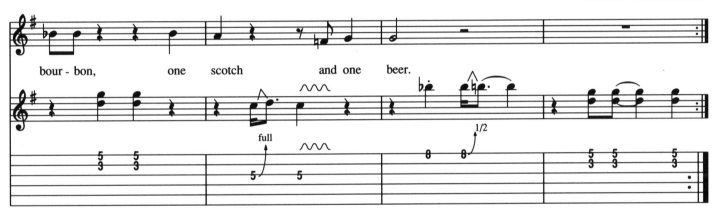

2nd Verse

Sung: Well my baby's been gone, she's been gone tonight
I ain't seen my baby since night before last.
I wanna get drunk, get her off a' my mind.
One bourbon, one scotch, and one beer

Spoken: And I sat there, gettin' high, stoned, knocked out,
And by that time, I looked on the wall,
At the old clock again, and by that time,
It was a quarter to two:
Last call for alcohol.
I said "Hey Mr. Bartender!"
"What do ya want?"

Sung: One bourbon, one scotch, and one beer

(repeat and fade)

Louise

By Chester Burnett

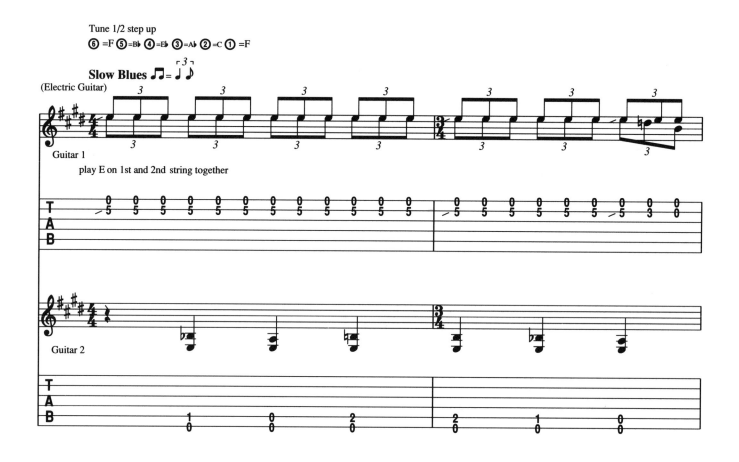

Verse

1. I said now,_ "look ah-here now, Lou-ise, the big boat's up the
2. I said now,_ "look ah-here now, Lou-ise, what some-one's doin' to

riv - er on a bank of sand. Nev - er strike the wa-ter God knows, the
me, Catch - ing my white perch- es, God knows, and

boat will nev-er land." I said: "Lou-ise, _____ you're the sweet-est girl I know.
dry-ing up my bones."

Caused me to walk _____ from Chi-ca-go, ___

to the Gulf of ___ Mex - i - co."

1st and 2nd string

to the Gulf of ___ Mex - i - co."

Spoken: Let's

I did-n't give up though, man; I kept on walk -in', try'n to find that wom- an.

Coda

Gulf of ____ Mex - i - co."

Maudie

By John Lee Hooker

Tune 1/2 step up
(Electric Guitar)

⑥ =F ⑤ =B♭ ④ =E♭ ③ =A♭ ② =C ① =F

Boogie ♩=108

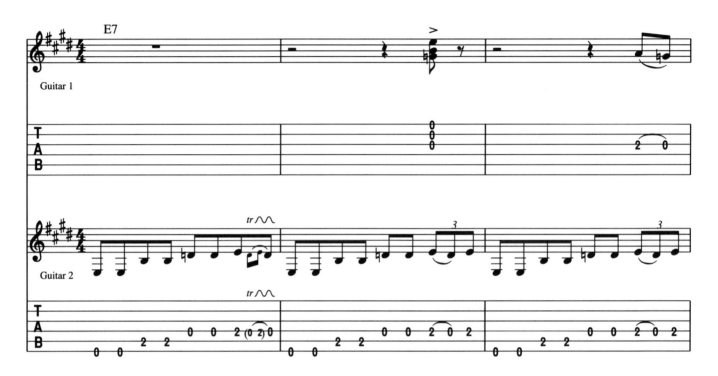

ba—by, I ___ love you.
why _ did you hurt me?

You've been gone so long, ___ cause I miss you so. _
I love you ba—by, you've been gone too long.

The Mighty Fire

By John Lee Hooker

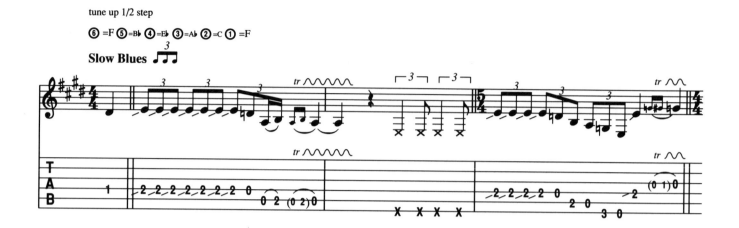

1. Nine - teen and thir - ty six, the migh - ty fire of Natch - ez, Miss - is - sip - pi.

2.,3.,4. *(See additional lyrics)*

(string bass accompaniment throughout)

(R.H.)
brush with 1st
finger

Nine - teen and thir - ty - six, people,__ the might - y fire of Natch - ez, Miss - is - sip - pi

They had a   big dance that night   and when the fire   broke out,

well, the   barn was down.   Lou - ise was there,   I - da

Mae was there;   she   was   my   heart.

To Coda $\bigoplus$ | 1. ,2.,3.

3rd time to instrumental   **Instrumental break**

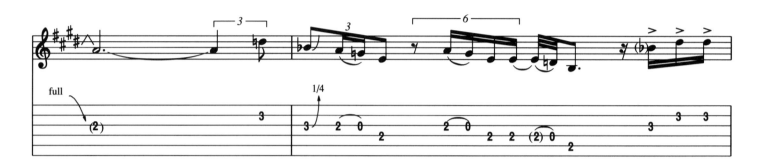

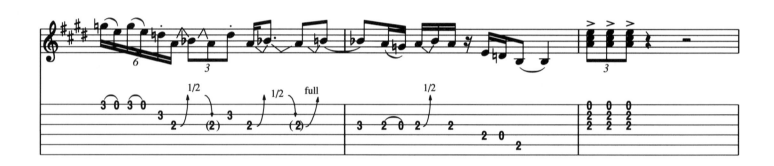

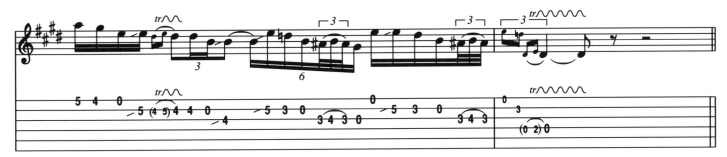

Coda

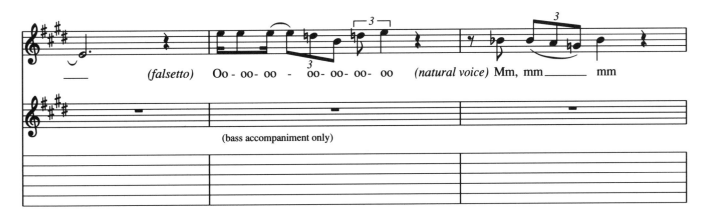

(falsetto) Oo - oo- oo - oo- oo- oo- oo   *(natural voice)* Mm, mm_____ mm

(bass accompaniment only)

Fine

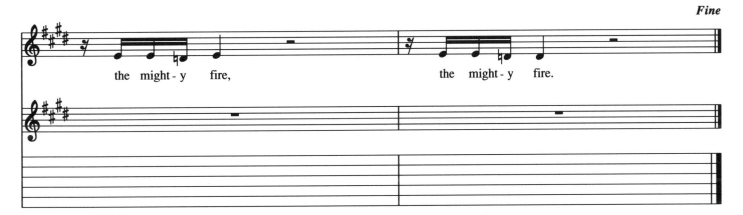

the might - y fire,   the might - y fire.

2nd verse
Saturday morning, I read the paper;
I saw Ida Mae's name.
I couldn't read no more.
The mighty fire, the mighty fire
of Natchez, Mississippi.

3rd verse
Ninetheen and thirty-six, people,
The place was full and jammed with people
when the fire broke out
Hm, Hm, Hm
Talkin' 'bout Natchez, Mississippi

(instrumental break)

4th verse
I'm talkin' 'bout Natchez, Mississippi,
Nineteen and thirty-six.
Louise was there, my girlfriend buddy
Ida Mae was there.
The Saturday morning
I bought myself a paper;
I read about the news.
I saw Ida Mae's name;
She went down in the mighty fire.
I felt so bad,
Ooo ---, Hm, Hm, Hm.
The mighty fire, the mighty fire.

My First Wife Left Me

By John Lee Hooker

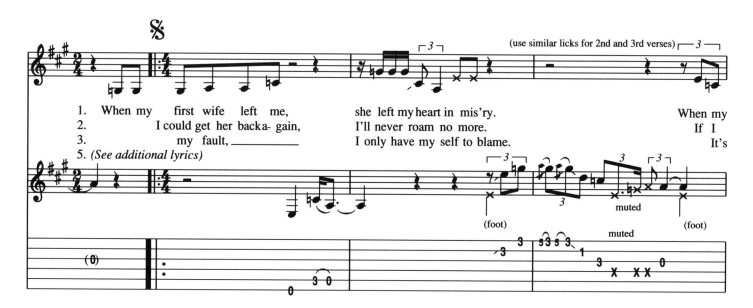

1. When my first wife left me, she left my heart in mis'ry. When my
2. I could get her back a- gain, I'll never roam no more. If I
3. my fault, _____ I only have my self to blame. It's
5. *(See additional lyrics)*

first wife left me, she left my heart in mis -'ry.
get her back a - gain boys, I'll nev - er roam no more.
my fault, it's my fault, boys I only have my - self to blame. _____

Ev–er since that day, boys
I had a good wife,
She would have been home right now

I don't think I'll ev – er love a- gain
but I did not treat her right.
If I'd hadn't want - ed ev-'ry wom - an that I'd seen

2. If
3. It's

4. I found out one thing:___ these wom- en don't mean you no good.

I found out one thing, peo- ple: ___ these wom- en don't mean you no good.

(foot)

You mis- treat a good girl for some wom- an, then she'll turn a- round and turn her back on

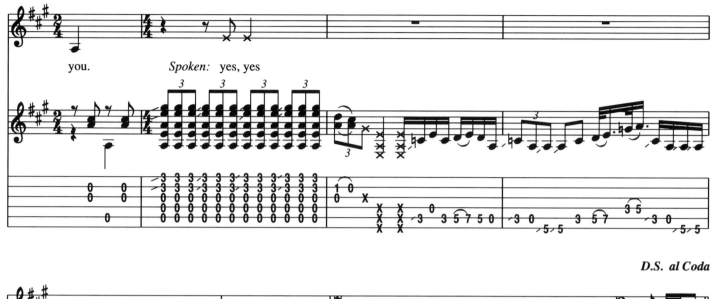

you. *Spoken:* yes, yes

D.S. al Coda

5. I'm hav- in' bad

Lord, I did not treat her right.

foot

4th verse
I'm havin' bad luck,
Havin' bad luck ever since she's been gone
Havin' bad luck, bad luck, bad luck
Ever since my baby's been gone
When she was at home, Lord
I did not treat her right.

Process

By John Lee Hooker

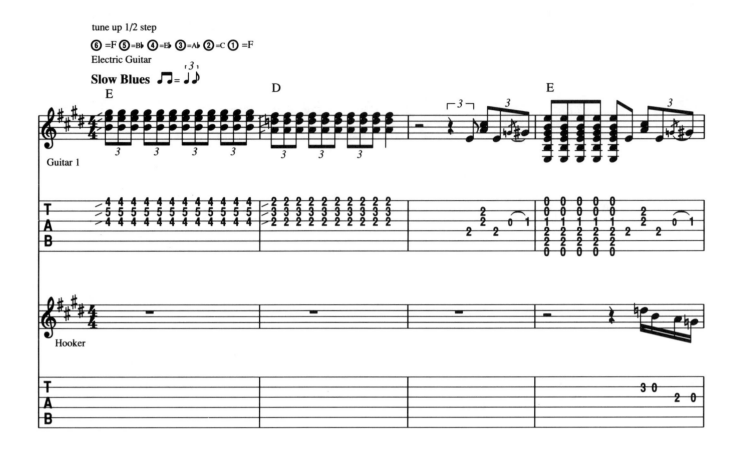

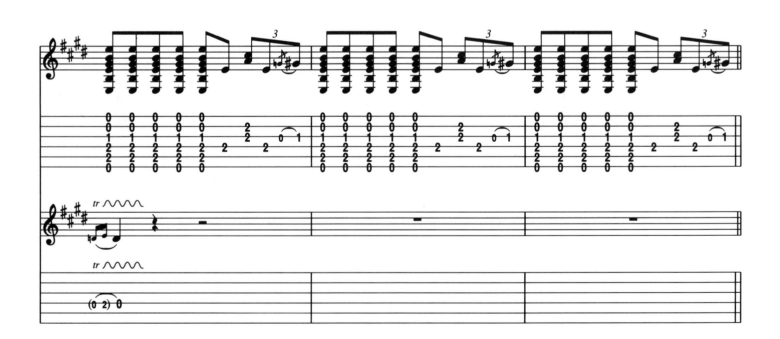

1.   Don't want no wom- an,   crazy 'bout a pro- cess head; __
2. She ain't got no mon - ey,   she on -ly has hair- do fare; __
3. *(See additional lyrics)*

Don't want no wom- an,   crazy 'bout a pro- cess head; __
she ain't got no mon -ey,   she on - ly has hair- do fare; __

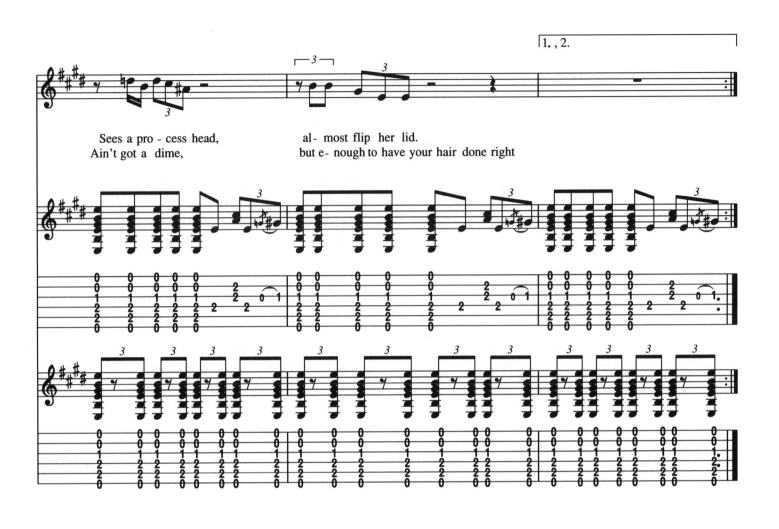

Sees a pro - cess head,   al- most flip her lid.

Ain't got a dime,   but e- nough to have your hair done right

Instrumental

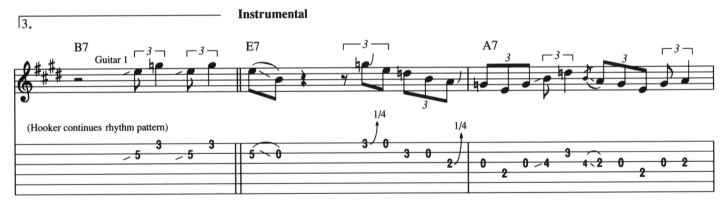

(Hooker continues rhythm pattern)

3rd verse
(yes, yes)
I had a fool one time,
Go crazy over processed heads;
Had a fool one time, go crazy over processed heads.
That no good woman, almost drove me insane.
(spoken) "Have mercy," she said.

(Instrumental break)

Stella Mae

By John Lee Hooker

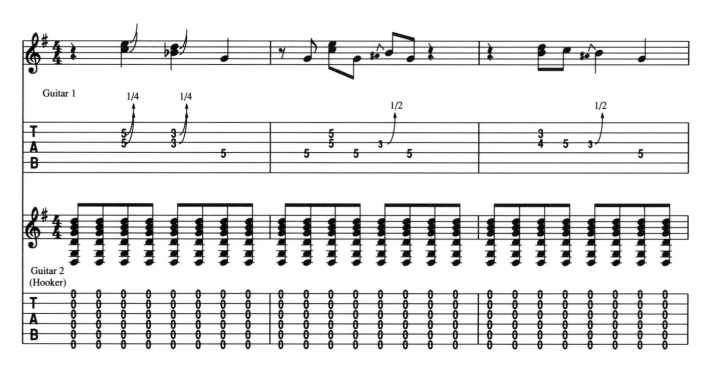

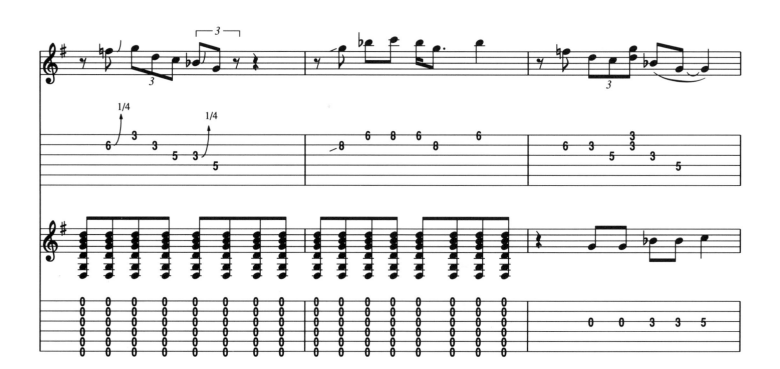

1. Stel - la Mae,   I love you,
you changed my drink,   to milk and creme.

2. Mae,
3.,4.,5. *See additional lyrics*

Guitar 2 continues rhythm pattern to accompany

singing:

ba – by.
I did it, I did it, just for you, 'cause I love _____

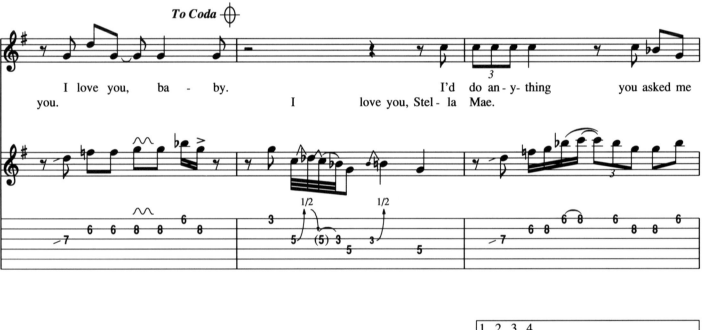

I love you, ba – by. I'd do an- y- thing you asked me
you. I love you, Stel - la Mae.

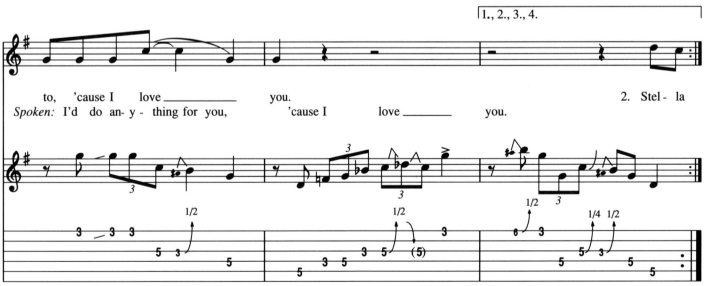

to, 'cause I love _____ you.
Spoken: I'd do an- y- thing for you, 'cause I love _____ you.
2. Stel - la

Instrumental Break
"Oh yeah"
Guitar 1 continue licks in similar style through break

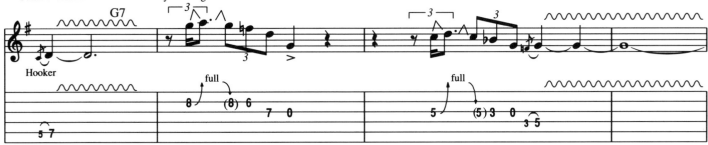

Hooker

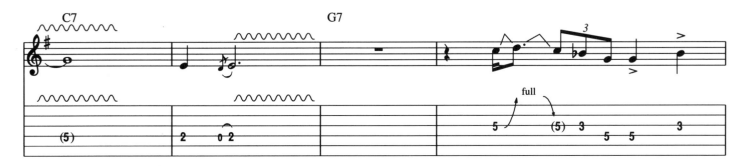

Ba - by!   (sung falsetto) Oo _____   Oo ___

Coda

Repeat and Fade

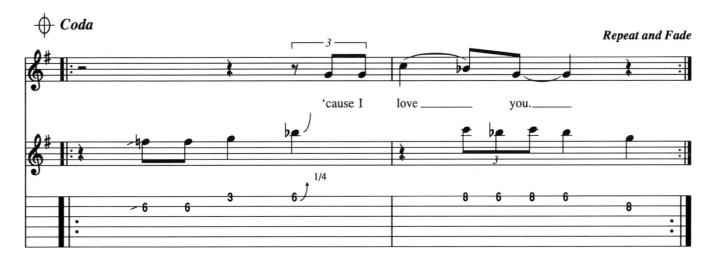

'cause I   love _____   you.___

3rd verse
Now, Stella Mae, if you told me to jump in the ocean,
I know I can't swim, but I'd try to do it just for you.
Because I love you, I love you, Stella Mae.

4th verse
Now, baby, you made me stop gambling;
You made me stop staying up all night long.
Now, Stella Mae, I did all these things, I did them just for you.
'Cause I love you, I love you, oh yeah.

5th verse
Now Stella Mae, if I had my choice for the whole round world,
I, I, baby, I'd tell you to be my choice.
'Cause I love you, 'Cause I love you, 'Cause I love you
(fade)

This Is It

By John Lee Hooker

Tune 1/2 step up

⑥ =F ⑤=B♭ ④=E♭ ③=A♭ ②=C ①=E♭

Medium Shuffle ♩=132

Guitar 1

(brush chord w/thumb)

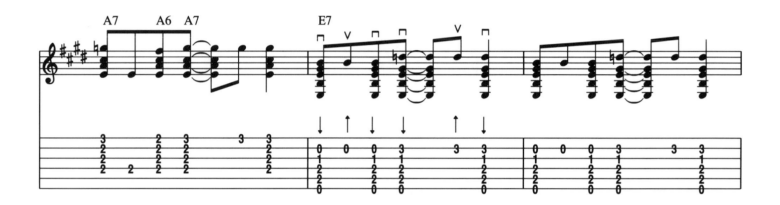

Chorus

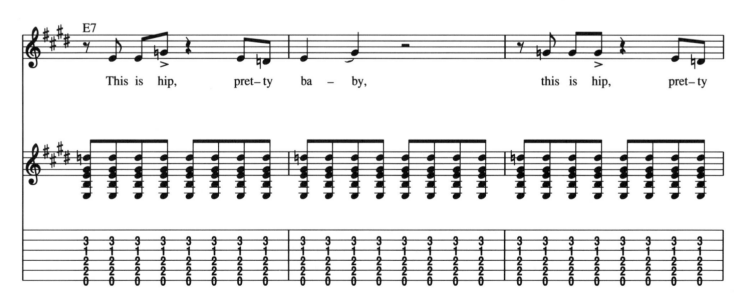

This is hip, pret–ty ba – by,   this is hip, pret–ty

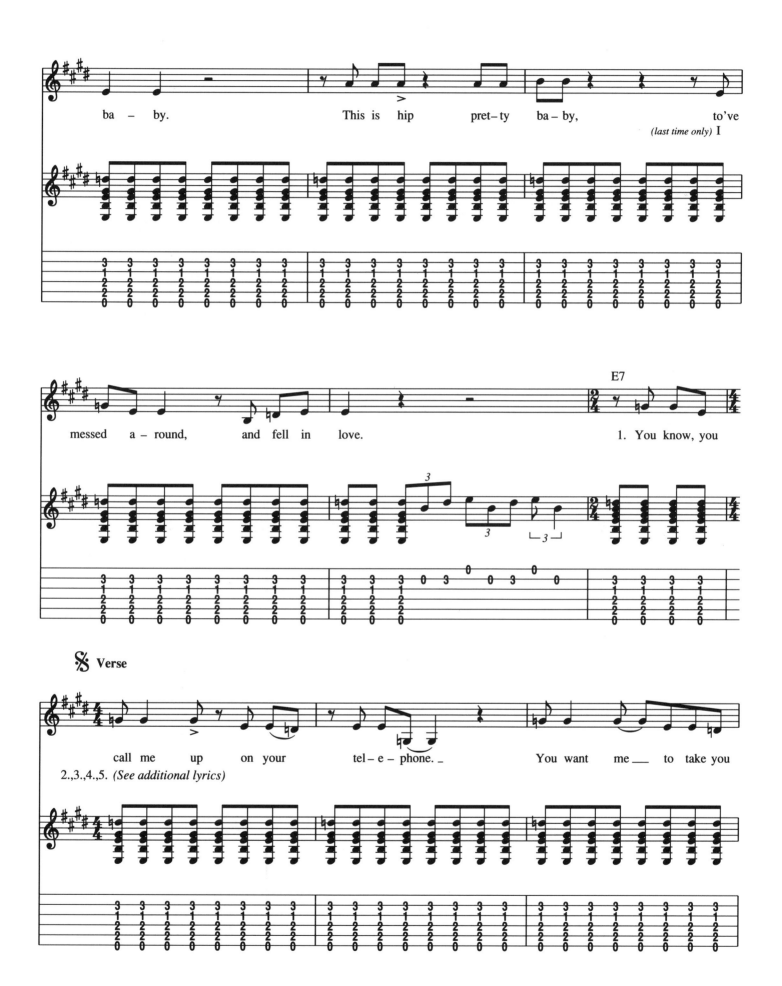

ba — by.   This is hip pret—ty ba—by,   to've

(last time only) I

messed a — round, and fell in love.

E7

1. You know, you

𝄋 Verse

call me up on your tel—e—phone. _ You want me _ to take you

2.,3.,4.,5. *(See additional lyrics)*

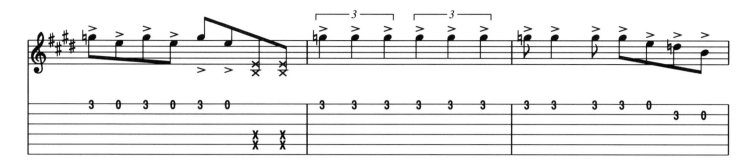

D.S. al Coda ⊕

⊕ *Coda*

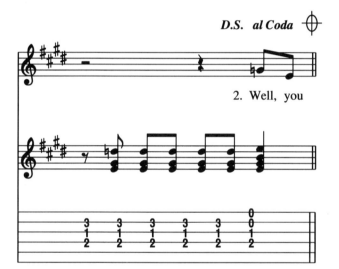

2. Well, you

Fine

E7

messed a– round   and fell in   love.

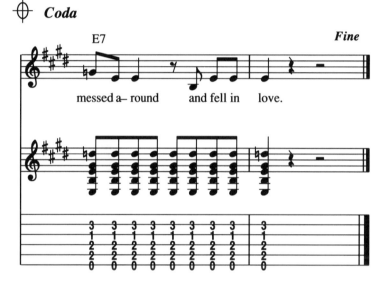

Additional Verses:

2) Well, you come to my house,
   And you dance with me.
   You hold me tight,
   And you kiss me, too.

Repeat Chorus

3) When you call me up,
   You talk a long time.
   You talk to me,
   Over your telephone.
   You tell me you're comin'
   Right over, baby

Repeat Chorus

4) When you dance with me,
   You rock me, too.
   You rock my soul,
   And I'm satisfied.

Repeat Chorus

5) That was a rockin' good way,
   You've been a rockin' good way,
   (Coda) I messed around and fell in love

Lyrics to the 4th verse
   When you call me up,
   You talk a long time.
   You talk to me,
   Over your telephone.
   You tell me you're comin'
   Right over, baby
   This is hip, pretty baby, *(3 times)*
   To mess around and fall in love

Lyrics to the 5th verse
   When you dance with me,
   You rock me, too.
   You rock my soul,
   And I'm satisfied.
   This is hip, pretty baby, *(3 times)*
   To mess around and fall in love

Lyrics to the 6th verse
   That was a rockin' good way,
   You've been a rockin' good way,
   You've been a rockin' good way,
   I messed around and fell in love

Wednesday Evening Blues

By John Lee Hooker

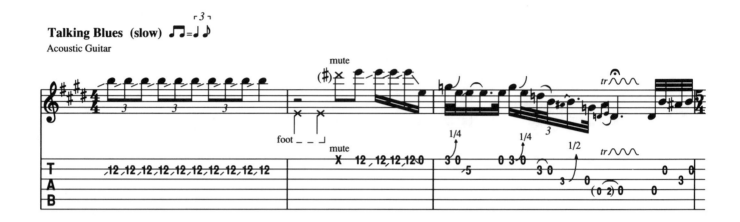

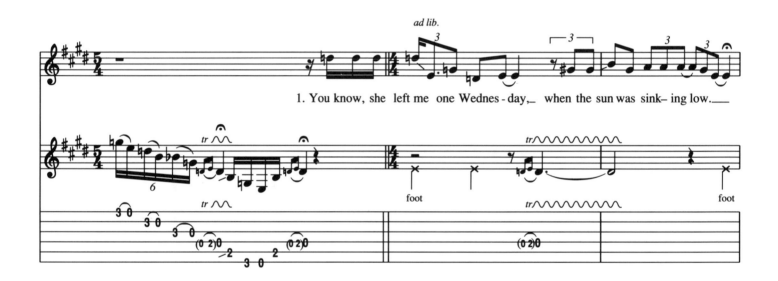

1. You know, she left me one Wednes-day,— when the sun was sink–ing low.—

Ooh, she left me that Wednes- day eve-ning, when the sun was sink- ing low.

when the   sun was __ sink–ing low.

Mm, __ mm, __ mm. __

foot

Mm,   mm,   mm   mm   mm   mm

Oh _____ oh ho ho. _____

sat down and told me...   *Spoken:* she said, "John – ny,   you can do a girl so bad,

(See additional narration)

and you're in love...."   I said, "Ba – by, please don't go home,

I have changed my mind.

That was one Wednes– day eve– ning

_____ when the sun was sink– ing low. ____

Mm __ mm __ mm. ____ Mm. _____ Mm, mm, ____ mm, ____ mm, ____

Narration #1

My baby told me, "I told you, Johnny, a long time ago.
If you don't stop your old way, I'm gonna leave you, baby.
You thought one thing: I love you too hard to leave you.
But now the day has come. You love me; I don't love you.
You did me so bad, you drove my love away.
But now, I'm leaving. Mm, mm, leaving..."

The day is Wednesday. Leaving on this day.
Every day, people, every day on Wednesday.

Narration #2

She said, "Johnny, you can do a girl so bad.
She can love you a length of time.
If you don't change your mind, the girl gets tired;
Her love goes away. But now I'm tired, "

Peace - Lovin' Man

By John Lee Hooker

Electric Guitar

2nd Guitar continues with similar licks throughout song

1. I'm a peace-lov-in' man
2. I see trou-ble babe, __
3. (See additional lyrics)

I don't want trou - ble;
way up yon - der,   a - head of me.
I'm a peace lov-in' man,
I bet- ter go now babe. __

I don't want trou - ble, ba - by.
I smell trou - ble, _____
I smell trou - ble, _____   I'd bet- ter go   now babe,
I   smell

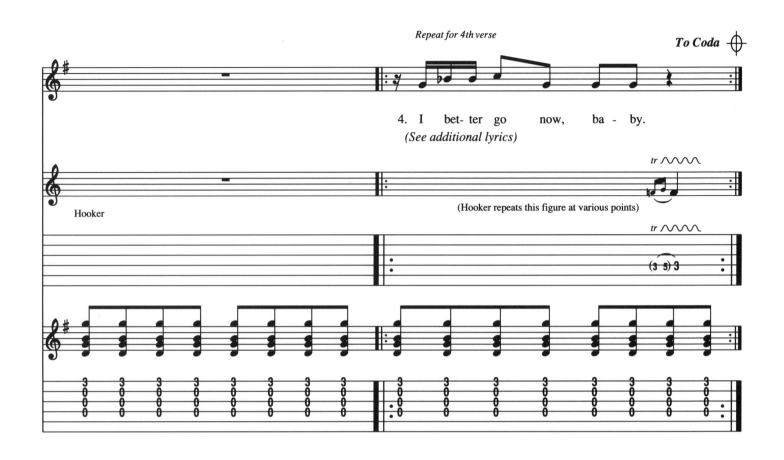

4. I bet-ter go now, ba-by.
(See additional lyrics)

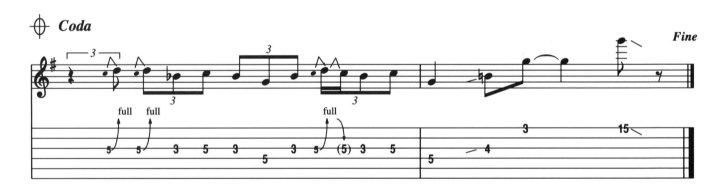

3rd verse
I don't want no trouble, baby.
I'm a peace-lover;
I'm a peace-lovin' man.
Oh yeah, now, baby,
I don't want trouble, baby.
All you did for me is made it hard.
I don't want trouble.
Oh, yeah.

(Instrumental)

4th verse
I better go now babe;
I don't want trouble.
I'm gonna leave you now, babe;
I don't want trouble, baby.
All done losin' everything I had, babe.
I don't want trouble,
I don't want trouble
I, I, I, I hate to leave, baby,
But I don't want trouble
I better go; I better go now, babe.
I, I, I, I, I, I, I don't want trouble, babe.
Goodbye, goodbye, babe.
Goodbye, baby.

To Coda (no vocal on Coda)

Tupelo

By John Lee Hooker

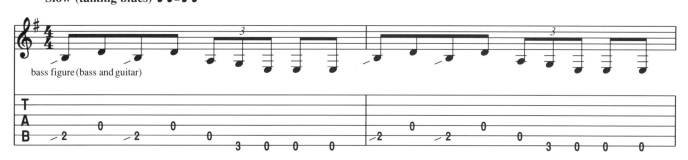

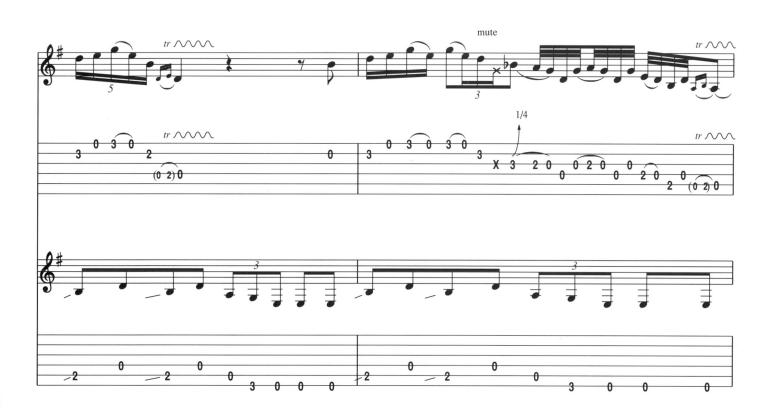

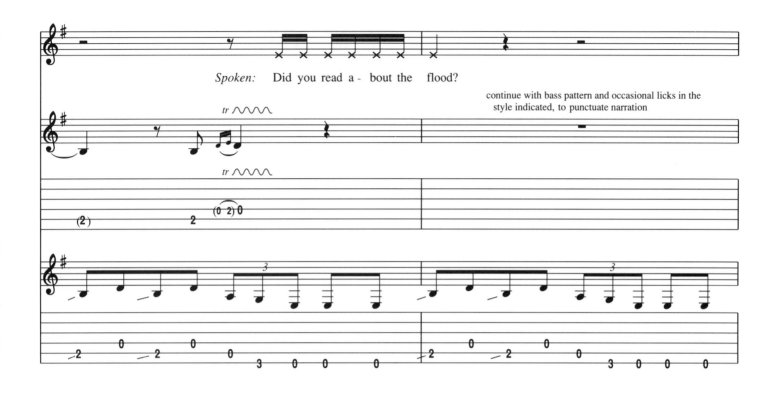

Spoken: Did you read a - bout the flood?

continue with bass pattern and occasional licks in the
style indicated, to punctuate narration

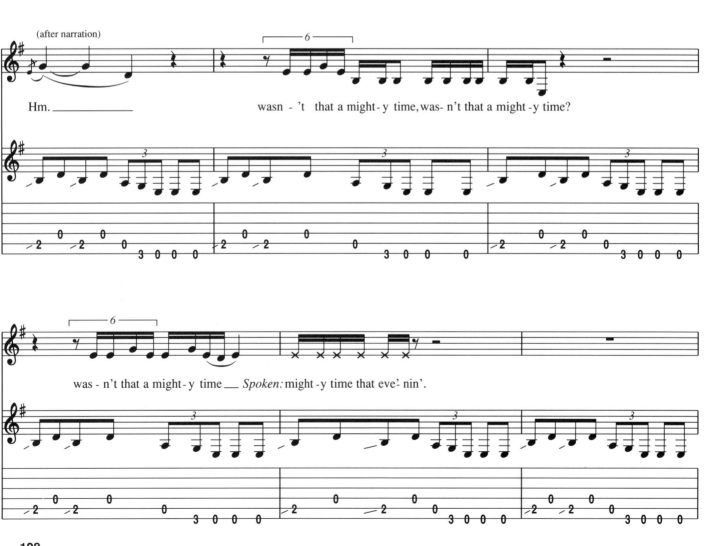

(after narration)

Hm. _____

wasn - 't that a might- y time, was- n't that a might -y time?

was - n't that a might- y time ___ Spoken: might -y time that eve- nin'.

Sung: It rained, both night and day. The poor peo-

-ple ___ had no place to go ___ Hm, Hm, a lit-tle town ___

___ *Spoken:* called Tu-pe-lo, Miss-iss-ip-pi I'll nev-er for-get it I

know you won't ei-ther

Play 3 times

Fine

Hm ___

109

NOTATION LEGEND

RECORDED VERSIONS
The Best Note-For-Note Transcriptions Available

ALL BOOKS INCLUDE TABLATURE